53 Low Salt Recipes for Home

By: Kelly Johnson

Table of Contents

- Grilled Lemon Herb Chicken
- Quinoa Salad with Vegetables
- Baked Salmon with Dill
- Roasted Vegetable Stir-Fry
- Turkey and Vegetable Skewers
- Spinach and Feta Stuffed Chicken Breast
- Shrimp and Avocado Salad
- Lemon Garlic Roasted Brussels Sprouts
- Mediterranean Chickpea Salad
- Baked Cod with Herbs
- Cucumber and Tomato Gazpacho
- Garlic and Herb Roasted Sweet Potatoes
- Lemon Thyme Grilled Shrimp
- Chicken and Vegetable Curry
- Zucchini Noodles with Pesto
- Roasted Red Pepper and Lentil Soup
- Herb-Roasted Turkey Breast
- Cauliflower Rice Pilaf
- Caprese Salad with Balsamic Glaze
- Lemon Basil Grilled Vegetables
- Baked Tilapia with Lemon and Herbs
- Chickpea and Spinach Stew
- Grilled Portobello Mushrooms

- Broccoli and Quinoa Casserole
- Greek Yogurt Chicken Salad
- Lemon Rosemary Roasted Potatoes
- Avocado and Black Bean Salad
- Herb Crusted Baked Chicken
- Ratatouille with Herbs de Provence
- Shrimp and Zucchini Skewers
- Lemon Garlic Roasted Asparagus
- Baked Eggplant Parmesan
- Herb-Marinated Grilled Tofu
- Tomato Basil Quinoa Pilaf
- Orange Glazed Grilled Chicken
- Cabbage and Apple Slaw
- Roasted Garlic Hummus
- Herb-Rubbed Pork Tenderloin
- Lemon Cilantro Quinoa
- Grilled Vegetable Wrap
- White Bean and Vegetable Soup
- Garlic and Herb Baked Cod
- Mediterranean Stuffed Bell Peppers
- Lemon Dill Salmon Burgers
- Roasted Butternut Squash Soup
- Rosemary Roasted Chicken Thighs
- Quinoa and Black Bean Stuffed Peppers
- Grilled Zucchini and Tomato Salad
- Baked Herb-Crusted Whitefish

- Spinach and Mushroom Frittata
- Lemon Garlic Shrimp Stir-Fry
- Roasted Brussels Sprouts and Quinoa Salad
- Herb-Marinated Grilled Lamb Chops

Grilled Lemon Herb Chicken

Ingredients:

- 4 boneless, skinless chicken breasts
- 2 lemons (juiced and zested)
- 3 tablespoons olive oil
- 2 cloves garlic, minced
- 1 teaspoon dried oregano
- 1 teaspoon dried thyme
- Salt and pepper to taste
- Fresh parsley for garnish

Instructions:

In a bowl, whisk together lemon juice, lemon zest, olive oil, minced garlic, dried oregano, dried thyme, salt, and pepper. This will be your marinade.

Place the chicken breasts in a shallow dish or a large zip-top plastic bag. Pour the marinade over the chicken, making sure each piece is well-coated. Seal the bag or cover the dish and refrigerate for at least 30 minutes to marinate. For more flavor, you can marinate it for up to 4 hours.

Preheat the grill to medium-high heat.

Remove the chicken from the marinade and let any excess drip off.

Grill the chicken breasts for about 6-8 minutes per side, or until the internal temperature reaches 165°F (74°C) and the chicken is no longer pink in the center. While grilling, baste the chicken with the remaining marinade to keep it moist and flavorful.

Once cooked, remove the chicken from the grill and let it rest for a few minutes. Garnish with fresh parsley and serve the grilled lemon herb chicken with your favorite side dishes, such as a quinoa salad or grilled vegetables.

This recipe delivers a burst of fresh and zesty flavors with the combination of lemon and herbs. Adjust the seasoning according to your taste preferences, and enjoy your delicious and healthy grilled chicken!

Quinoa Salad with Vegetables

Ingredients:

For the Salad:

- 1 cup quinoa, rinsed
- 2 cups water or vegetable broth
- 1 cucumber, diced
- 1 bell pepper (any color), diced
- 1 cup cherry tomatoes, halved
- 1/2 red onion, finely chopped
- 1/4 cup fresh parsley, chopped
- 1/4 cup feta cheese, crumbled (optional)
- 1/4 cup black olives, sliced (optional)

For the Dressing:

- 1/4 cup extra-virgin olive oil
- 2 tablespoons balsamic vinegar
- 1 teaspoon Dijon mustard
- 1 clove garlic, minced
- Salt and pepper to taste

Instructions:

In a medium saucepan, combine quinoa and water or vegetable broth. Bring to a boil, then reduce heat to low, cover, and simmer for 15 minutes, or until the quinoa is cooked and the liquid is absorbed. Remove from heat and let it sit, covered, for 5 minutes. Fluff with a fork and allow it to cool.

In a large bowl, combine the cooled quinoa, diced cucumber, diced bell pepper, cherry tomatoes, red onion, and chopped parsley.

In a small bowl, whisk together the olive oil, balsamic vinegar, Dijon mustard, minced garlic, salt, and pepper to make the dressing.

Pour the dressing over the quinoa and vegetables. Toss everything together until well combined.

If using, add crumbled feta cheese and sliced black olives. Toss gently to incorporate.

Taste the salad and adjust the seasoning if needed.

Chill the quinoa salad in the refrigerator for at least 30 minutes to allow the flavors to meld.

Before serving, give the salad a final toss and garnish with additional parsley, if desired.

This Quinoa Salad with Vegetables is a nutritious and flavorful dish that can be enjoyed as a side or a light main course. Feel free to customize it by adding your favorite vegetables or protein sources. Enjoy!

Baked Salmon with Dill

Ingredients:

- 4 salmon fillets
- Salt and pepper, to taste
- 2 tablespoons olive oil
- 2 tablespoons fresh dill, chopped
- 2 cloves garlic, minced
- 1 lemon, sliced for garnish
- Lemon wedges for serving

Instructions:

Preheat your oven to 375°F (190°C).

Pat the salmon fillets dry with paper towels. Season both sides with salt and pepper.

In a small bowl, mix together the olive oil, chopped dill, and minced garlic to create the marinade.

Place the salmon fillets on a baking sheet lined with parchment paper or lightly greased.

Brush the salmon fillets with the dill and garlic marinade, ensuring they are well coated.

Place a slice or two of lemon on top of each fillet for added flavor.

Bake the salmon in the preheated oven for about 15-20 minutes or until the salmon flakes easily with a fork. The exact cooking time will depend on the thickness of your salmon fillets.

If desired, you can broil the salmon for an additional 2-3 minutes to get a golden brown crust on top.

Remove the salmon from the oven, garnish with additional fresh dill if desired, and serve hot.

Serve the baked salmon with lemon wedges on the side for squeezing over the fish.

This Baked Salmon with Dill is not only easy to prepare but also full of flavor. The combination of dill, garlic, and lemon enhances the natural taste of the salmon. Enjoy your delicious and healthy meal!

Roasted Vegetable Stir-Fry

Ingredients:

For the Roasted Vegetables:

- 2 cups broccoli florets
- 1 red bell pepper, sliced
- 1 yellow bell pepper, sliced
- 1 zucchini, sliced
- 1 yellow squash, sliced
- 1 carrot, julienned
- 2 tablespoons olive oil
- Salt and pepper to taste
- 1 teaspoon dried thyme
- 1 teaspoon paprika

For the Stir-Fry Sauce:

- 3 tablespoons soy sauce (or tamari for a gluten-free option)
- 2 tablespoons hoisin sauce
- 1 tablespoon rice vinegar
- 1 tablespoon honey or maple syrup
- 1 teaspoon sesame oil
- 2 cloves garlic, minced
- 1 teaspoon ginger, grated

For Serving:

- Cooked brown rice or quinoa

Instructions:

Preheat your oven to 425°F (220°C).

In a large mixing bowl, combine broccoli florets, sliced red and yellow bell peppers, zucchini, yellow squash, and julienned carrot.

Drizzle the olive oil over the vegetables and season with salt, pepper, dried thyme, and paprika. Toss until the vegetables are evenly coated.

Spread the seasoned vegetables on a baking sheet in a single layer.

Roast the vegetables in the preheated oven for about 20-25 minutes or until they are tender and slightly browned, stirring halfway through.

While the vegetables are roasting, prepare the stir-fry sauce. In a small bowl, whisk together soy sauce, hoisin sauce, rice vinegar, honey or maple syrup, sesame oil, minced garlic, and grated ginger.

Once the vegetables are roasted, heat a large wok or skillet over medium-high heat.

Add the roasted vegetables to the wok or skillet and pour the stir-fry sauce over them.

Stir-fry for an additional 3-5 minutes, ensuring that the vegetables are well-coated in the sauce and heated through.

Serve the roasted vegetable stir-fry over cooked brown rice or quinoa.

This Roasted Vegetable Stir-Fry is a colorful and flavorful dish that's both healthy and satisfying. Feel free to customize the vegetable selection based on your preferences. Enjoy your delicious stir-fry!

Turkey and Vegetable Skewers

Ingredients:

For the Turkey Marinade:

- 1 pound (about 450g) turkey breast, cut into cubes
- 2 tablespoons olive oil
- 2 tablespoons soy sauce
- 1 tablespoon honey or maple syrup
- 1 teaspoon Dijon mustard
- 2 cloves garlic, minced
- 1 teaspoon dried thyme
- Salt and pepper to taste

For the Vegetable Skewers:

- Cherry tomatoes
- Bell peppers (any color), cut into chunks
- Red onion, cut into wedges
- Zucchini, sliced

For Serving:

- Fresh parsley, chopped (optional)
- Lemon wedges

Instructions:

In a bowl, whisk together the olive oil, soy sauce, honey or maple syrup, Dijon mustard, minced garlic, dried thyme, salt, and pepper to create the turkey marinade.

Add the turkey cubes to the marinade, ensuring they are well-coated. Cover the bowl and refrigerate for at least 30 minutes to marinate. You can marinate longer for more flavor, up to 4 hours.

Preheat your grill or grill pan to medium-high heat.

While the turkey is marinating, soak wooden skewers in water for about 20-30 minutes to prevent them from burning on the grill.

Thread the marinated turkey cubes onto the skewers, alternating with the cherry tomatoes, bell peppers, red onion, and zucchini.

Brush the vegetable skewers with a little extra marinade for added flavor.

Grill the skewers for about 8-10 minutes, turning occasionally, until the turkey is cooked through and the vegetables are tender and slightly charred.

Remove the skewers from the grill and let them rest for a few minutes.

Sprinkle chopped fresh parsley over the skewers, if desired.

Serve the Turkey and Vegetable Skewers with lemon wedges on the side.

These Turkey and Vegetable Skewers are a tasty and healthy option for a summer barbecue or a quick weeknight meal. Enjoy!

Spinach and Feta Stuffed Chicken Breast

Ingredients:

- 4 boneless, skinless chicken breasts
- Salt and black pepper to taste
- 2 cups fresh spinach, chopped
- 1 cup feta cheese, crumbled
- 2 tablespoons olive oil
- 2 cloves garlic, minced
- 1 teaspoon dried oregano
- 1 teaspoon dried thyme
- 1 teaspoon paprika
- Toothpicks or kitchen twine (optional)

Instructions:

Preheat your oven to 375°F (190°C).

Season both sides of each chicken breast with salt and black pepper.

In a skillet, heat olive oil over medium heat. Add minced garlic and sauté for about 1 minute until fragrant.

Add chopped spinach to the skillet and cook until wilted, about 2-3 minutes. Remove the skillet from heat and let the spinach cool slightly.

In a bowl, combine the sautéed spinach, crumbled feta cheese, dried oregano, dried thyme, and paprika. Mix well.

Butterfly each chicken breast by slicing horizontally through the center, being careful not to cut all the way through.

Stuff each chicken breast with the spinach and feta mixture, pressing the edges together to seal. You can use toothpicks or kitchen twine to secure if needed. Season the outside of the stuffed chicken breasts with a little more salt, pepper, and paprika.

Heat a large oven-safe skillet over medium-high heat. Add a bit of olive oil if necessary.

Sear the stuffed chicken breasts for 2-3 minutes on each side until golden brown.

Transfer the skillet to the preheated oven and bake for about 20-25 minutes or until the internal temperature of the chicken reaches 165°F (74°C).

Remove from the oven and let the chicken rest for a few minutes before serving. Optionally, garnish with additional fresh herbs and serve with your favorite side dishes.

These Spinach and Feta Stuffed Chicken Breasts make for an elegant and flavorful dish that's sure to impress. Enjoy!

Shrimp and Avocado Salad

Ingredients:

For the Salad:

- 1 pound (about 450g) large shrimp, peeled and deveined
- 1 tablespoon olive oil
- Salt and black pepper to taste
- 1 teaspoon smoked paprika
- 6 cups mixed salad greens (e.g., arugula, spinach, or lettuce)
- 1 cup cherry tomatoes, halved
- 1 cucumber, diced
- 2 avocados, diced
- 1/4 cup red onion, thinly sliced
- 1/4 cup fresh cilantro or parsley, chopped

For the Dressing:

- 3 tablespoons olive oil
- 2 tablespoons lime juice
- 1 clove garlic, minced
- 1 teaspoon honey or maple syrup
- Salt and black pepper to taste

Instructions:

Preheat a large skillet over medium-high heat.

In a bowl, toss the shrimp with olive oil, salt, black pepper, and smoked paprika until well-coated.

Cook the shrimp in the preheated skillet for 2-3 minutes per side or until they are opaque and cooked through. Remove from heat and set aside.

In a large salad bowl, combine the mixed salad greens, cherry tomatoes, diced cucumber, diced avocados, sliced red onion, and chopped cilantro or parsley.

In a small bowl, whisk together the olive oil, lime juice, minced garlic, honey or maple syrup, salt, and black pepper to create the dressing.

Add the cooked shrimp to the salad, drizzle the dressing over the top, and gently toss everything together until well combined.

Serve the Shrimp and Avocado Salad immediately, garnished with additional cilantro or parsley if desired.

This Shrimp and Avocado Salad is not only light and refreshing but also packed with flavors. It makes for a perfect meal on its own or a delightful appetizer. Enjoy!

Lemon Garlic Roasted Brussels Sprouts

Ingredients:

- 1 pound (about 450g) Brussels sprouts, trimmed and halved
- 3 tablespoons olive oil
- 3 cloves garlic, minced
- Zest of 1 lemon
- 2 tablespoons fresh lemon juice
- Salt and black pepper to taste
- Optional: Parmesan cheese for garnish

Instructions:

Preheat your oven to 400°F (200°C).

In a large bowl, toss the halved Brussels sprouts with olive oil, minced garlic, lemon zest, and lemon juice. Ensure that the Brussels sprouts are well coated.

Season the Brussels sprouts with salt and black pepper to taste. Toss again to distribute the seasoning evenly.

Spread the Brussels sprouts in a single layer on a baking sheet lined with parchment paper or lightly greased.

Roast in the preheated oven for about 20-25 minutes or until the Brussels sprouts are golden brown and crispy on the edges. Be sure to stir or shake the pan halfway through the cooking time for even roasting.

Remove the roasted Brussels sprouts from the oven and transfer them to a serving dish.

Optional: Garnish with freshly grated Parmesan cheese for added flavor.

Serve the Lemon Garlic Roasted Brussels Sprouts hot as a side dish or a delicious snack.

This recipe combines the earthy flavor of Brussels sprouts with the bright and zesty combination of lemon and garlic. It's a simple and tasty way to enjoy this nutritious vegetable. Enjoy!

Mediterranean Chickpea Salad

Ingredients:

For the Salad:

- 2 cans (15 ounces each) chickpeas, drained and rinsed
- 1 cucumber, diced
- 1 cup cherry tomatoes, halved
- 1/2 red onion, finely chopped
- 1/2 cup Kalamata olives, pitted and sliced
- 1/2 cup crumbled feta cheese
- 1/4 cup fresh parsley, chopped

For the Dressing:

- 1/4 cup extra-virgin olive oil
- 2 tablespoons red wine vinegar
- 1 clove garlic, minced
- 1 teaspoon dried oregano
- Salt and black pepper to taste

Instructions:

In a large bowl, combine the chickpeas, diced cucumber, cherry tomatoes, chopped red onion, sliced Kalamata olives, crumbled feta cheese, and chopped fresh parsley.

In a small bowl or jar, whisk together the extra-virgin olive oil, red wine vinegar, minced garlic, dried oregano, salt, and black pepper to create the dressing.

Pour the dressing over the chickpea mixture and toss everything together until well coated.

Allow the Mediterranean Chickpea Salad to sit in the refrigerator for at least 30 minutes before serving to allow the flavors to meld.

Just before serving, give the salad a final toss and adjust the seasoning if needed.

Optional: Garnish with additional fresh parsley and a sprinkle of feta cheese.

Serve the Mediterranean Chickpea Salad as a refreshing side dish or a light meal on its own.

This salad is not only vibrant and full of Mediterranean flavors but also packed with protein and nutrients from the chickpeas. Enjoy!

Baked Cod with Herbs

Ingredients:

- 4 cod fillets (about 6 ounces each)
- 2 tablespoons olive oil
- 2 tablespoons fresh parsley, chopped
- 1 tablespoon fresh dill, chopped
- 1 tablespoon fresh thyme, chopped
- 2 cloves garlic, minced
- Zest of 1 lemon
- Juice of 1 lemon
- Salt and black pepper to taste
- Lemon wedges for serving

Instructions:

Preheat your oven to 400°F (200°C).

Pat the cod fillets dry with paper towels and place them in a baking dish lightly greased with olive oil.

In a small bowl, mix together olive oil, chopped parsley, chopped dill, chopped thyme, minced garlic, lemon zest, and lemon juice to create the herb mixture.

Brush the herb mixture over the top of each cod fillet, ensuring they are well coated. Season with salt and black pepper.

Bake the cod in the preheated oven for about 12-15 minutes or until the fish is opaque and flakes easily with a fork.

If desired, you can broil the cod for an additional 2-3 minutes to get a golden brown crust on top.

Remove the baked cod from the oven and let it rest for a few minutes.

Serve the Baked Cod with Herbs with lemon wedges on the side.

This Baked Cod with Herbs is a light and healthy dish with a burst of fresh flavors. It pairs well with a side of steamed vegetables, quinoa, or a simple green salad. Enjoy your delicious and nutritious meal!

Cucumber and Tomato Gazpacho

Ingredients:

- 4 large tomatoes, diced
- 2 cucumbers, peeled and diced
- 1 bell pepper (red or yellow), diced
- 1 small red onion, finely chopped
- 2 cloves garlic, minced
- 3 cups tomato juice
- 1/4 cup red wine vinegar
- 1/4 cup extra-virgin olive oil
- 1 teaspoon sugar (optional, to balance acidity)
- Salt and black pepper to taste
- 1 teaspoon ground cumin (optional, for added flavor)
- Fresh basil or cilantro for garnish
- Croutons (optional, for serving)

Instructions:

In a blender or food processor, combine diced tomatoes, cucumbers, bell pepper, red onion, and minced garlic.

Blend the vegetables until smooth. If necessary, work in batches.

Pour the blended mixture into a large bowl.

Add tomato juice, red wine vinegar, and extra-virgin olive oil to the bowl. Stir to combine.

Season the gazpacho with sugar (if using), salt, black pepper, and ground cumin. Adjust the seasoning according to your taste preferences.

Chill the gazpacho in the refrigerator for at least 2 hours, allowing the flavors to meld.

Before serving, give the gazpacho a good stir. If it has thickened too much, you can adjust the consistency by adding a little more tomato juice.

Ladle the chilled Cucumber and Tomato Gazpacho into bowls.

Garnish with fresh basil or cilantro and serve with croutons if desired.

This Cucumber and Tomato Gazpacho is a light and refreshing soup, perfect for warm days. It's a delightful way to enjoy the vibrant flavors of summer vegetables. Enjoy!

Garlic and Herb Roasted Sweet Potatoes

Ingredients:

- 3 large sweet potatoes, peeled and cut into cubes
- 3 tablespoons olive oil
- 3 cloves garlic, minced
- 1 teaspoon dried thyme
- 1 teaspoon dried rosemary
- 1 teaspoon dried oregano
- Salt and black pepper to taste
- Fresh parsley, chopped (optional, for garnish)

Instructions:

Preheat your oven to 400°F (200°C).

In a large bowl, toss the sweet potato cubes with olive oil, minced garlic, dried thyme, dried rosemary, dried oregano, salt, and black pepper. Ensure that the sweet potatoes are well coated with the herb mixture.

Spread the seasoned sweet potatoes in a single layer on a baking sheet lined with parchment paper or lightly greased.

Roast the sweet potatoes in the preheated oven for about 25-30 minutes or until they are golden brown and tender, stirring halfway through for even cooking.

Once the sweet potatoes are roasted to your liking, remove them from the oven.

Transfer the roasted sweet potatoes to a serving dish.

Optional: Garnish with fresh chopped parsley for added freshness.

Serve the Garlic and Herb Roasted Sweet Potatoes as a side dish with your favorite protein.

These roasted sweet potatoes are packed with flavor from the garlic and a medley of herbs, making them a delightful and nutritious side dish. Enjoy!

Lemon Thyme Grilled Shrimp

Ingredients:

- 1 pound large shrimp, peeled and deveined
- Zest of 1 lemon
- Juice of 1 lemon
- 2 tablespoons fresh thyme leaves, chopped
- 3 cloves garlic, minced
- 3 tablespoons olive oil
- Salt and black pepper to taste
- Lemon wedges for serving

Instructions:

In a bowl, combine the peeled and deveined shrimp with lemon zest, lemon juice, chopped thyme leaves, minced garlic, olive oil, salt, and black pepper. Toss to ensure the shrimp are evenly coated. Allow the shrimp to marinate for at least 15-30 minutes.
Preheat your grill to medium-high heat.
Thread the marinated shrimp onto skewers, ensuring they are evenly spaced.
Place the shrimp skewers on the preheated grill and cook for 2-3 minutes per side or until the shrimp are opaque and have grill marks.
Remove the shrimp skewers from the grill and transfer them to a serving plate.
Optional: Drizzle any remaining marinade over the grilled shrimp for extra flavor.
Serve the Lemon Thyme Grilled Shrimp hot with lemon wedges on the side for squeezing over the shrimp.

This Lemon Thyme Grilled Shrimp recipe offers a perfect balance of citrusy and herby flavors. It's a quick and easy dish that's perfect for a light meal or as part of a summer barbecue. Enjoy!

Chicken and Vegetable Curry

Ingredients:

- 1.5 pounds (about 680g) boneless, skinless chicken thighs, cut into bite-sized pieces
- 2 tablespoons vegetable oil
- 1 large onion, finely chopped
- 3 cloves garlic, minced
- 1 tablespoon ginger, grated
- 2 tablespoons curry powder
- 1 teaspoon ground cumin
- 1 teaspoon ground coriander
- 1/2 teaspoon turmeric
- 1/2 teaspoon chili powder (adjust to taste)
- 1 can (14 ounces) diced tomatoes
- 1 can (14 ounces) coconut milk
- 2 cups mixed vegetables (e.g., bell peppers, carrots, peas)
- Salt and pepper to taste
- Fresh cilantro, chopped (for garnish)
- Cooked rice or naan bread (for serving)

Instructions:

In a large skillet or Dutch oven, heat the vegetable oil over medium heat. Add the chopped onions to the pan and sauté until they become soft and translucent.

Add the minced garlic and grated ginger to the onions. Sauté for an additional 1-2 minutes until fragrant.

Push the onion mixture to the side of the pan and add the chicken pieces. Brown the chicken on all sides.

Once the chicken is browned, add the curry powder, ground cumin, ground coriander, turmeric, and chili powder. Stir well to coat the chicken and onions with the spices.

Pour in the diced tomatoes (with their juice) and coconut milk. Stir to combine all the ingredients.

Add the mixed vegetables to the curry mixture. Season with salt and pepper to taste.

Bring the curry to a simmer, then reduce the heat to low. Cover and let it simmer for about 20-25 minutes, or until the chicken is cooked through and the vegetables are tender.

Taste and adjust the seasoning if needed.

Serve the Chicken and Vegetable Curry over cooked rice or with naan bread.

Garnish with chopped fresh cilantro before serving.

This Chicken and Vegetable Curry is rich, flavorful, and perfect for a comforting meal. Adjust the spice level according to your preferences, and enjoy it with your favorite accompaniment.

Zucchini Noodles with Pesto

Ingredients:

For the Pesto Sauce:

- 2 cups fresh basil leaves, packed
- 1/2 cup grated Parmesan cheese
- 1/2 cup pine nuts or walnuts
- 2 cloves garlic, minced
- 1/2 cup extra-virgin olive oil
- Salt and black pepper to taste
- Juice of 1 lemon (optional)

For the Zucchini Noodles:

- 4 medium-sized zucchini, spiralized into noodles
- 1 tablespoon olive oil
- Cherry tomatoes, halved (optional, for garnish)
- Grated Parmesan cheese (optional, for garnish)

Instructions:

For the Pesto Sauce:

In a food processor, combine the basil leaves, grated Parmesan cheese, pine nuts or walnuts, and minced garlic.
Pulse until the ingredients are finely chopped.

With the food processor running, slowly drizzle in the olive oil until the pesto reaches your desired consistency.

Season the pesto with salt and black pepper to taste. If desired, add the juice of 1 lemon for a citrusy kick. Pulse again to combine.

Taste and adjust the seasoning as needed.

For the Zucchini Noodles:

Spiralize the zucchini into noodles using a spiralizer.

Heat olive oil in a large pan over medium heat.

Add the zucchini noodles to the pan and sauté for 2-3 minutes or until they are just tender. Be careful not to overcook, as zucchini noodles can become mushy.

Once the zucchini noodles are cooked, remove them from the heat.

Toss the zucchini noodles with the prepared pesto sauce until evenly coated.

Garnish with halved cherry tomatoes and grated Parmesan cheese if desired.

Serve the Zucchini Noodles with Pesto immediately.

This Zucchini Noodles with Pesto recipe is a light and flavorful alternative to traditional pasta dishes. It's a great way to enjoy a healthy and low-carb meal. Enjoy!

Roasted Red Pepper and Lentil Soup

Ingredients:

- 2 red bell peppers, halved and seeds removed
- 1 cup dry red lentils, rinsed and drained
- 1 onion, chopped
- 3 cloves garlic, minced
- 1 carrot, peeled and chopped
- 1 celery stalk, chopped
- 1 can (14 ounces) diced tomatoes
- 4 cups vegetable broth
- 1 teaspoon ground cumin
- 1 teaspoon smoked paprika
- 1/2 teaspoon ground coriander
- 1/2 teaspoon dried thyme
- Salt and black pepper to taste
- 2 tablespoons olive oil
- Fresh parsley, chopped (for garnish)
- Greek yogurt or coconut milk (optional, for serving)

Instructions:

Preheat your oven's broiler.

Place the halved red bell peppers on a baking sheet, skin side up.

Broil the peppers for 8-10 minutes or until the skin is charred and blistered.

Remove the peppers from the oven, place them in a bowl, and cover with plastic wrap. Let them steam for about 10 minutes.

Peel the skin off the roasted peppers and chop them into smaller pieces.

In a large pot, heat olive oil over medium heat. Add chopped onion, garlic, carrot, and celery. Sauté until the vegetables are softened.

Add the chopped roasted red peppers, rinsed red lentils, diced tomatoes, vegetable broth, cumin, smoked paprika, ground coriander, dried thyme, salt, and black pepper to the pot. Stir well to combine.

Bring the soup to a boil, then reduce the heat to low, cover, and simmer for about 20-25 minutes or until the lentils are tender.

Use an immersion blender to blend the soup until smooth. Alternatively, transfer the soup in batches to a blender, blend until smooth, and return to the pot.

Taste and adjust the seasoning if needed.

Serve the Roasted Red Pepper and Lentil Soup hot, garnished with fresh chopped parsley. Optionally, swirl in a dollop of Greek yogurt or coconut milk before serving.

This Roasted Red Pepper and Lentil Soup is not only delicious but also packed with nutrients. It's a comforting and satisfying soup that's perfect for cooler days. Enjoy!

Herb-Roasted Turkey Breast

Ingredients:

- 1 bone-in, skin-on turkey breast (about 4-5 pounds)
- 4 tablespoons unsalted butter, softened
- 2 tablespoons fresh herbs (such as rosemary, thyme, and sage), finely chopped
- 3 cloves garlic, minced
- 1 teaspoon dried oregano
- 1 teaspoon dried thyme
- 1 teaspoon dried rosemary
- Salt and black pepper to taste
- 1 cup chicken or turkey broth
- 1 onion, quartered
- 2 carrots, peeled and cut into chunks
- 2 celery stalks, cut into chunks
- Olive oil for coating

Instructions:

Preheat your oven to 325°F (163°C).

In a small bowl, mix together the softened butter, fresh herbs, minced garlic, dried oregano, dried thyme, dried rosemary, salt, and black pepper. This will be your herb butter.

Pat the turkey breast dry with paper towels. Gently lift the skin from the turkey breast and rub half of the herb butter directly onto the meat.

Place quartered onions, carrot chunks, and celery chunks in the bottom of a roasting pan.

Place the turkey breast, skin-side up, on top of the vegetables in the roasting pan.

Coat the skin with olive oil and rub the remaining herb butter over the skin.

Season the skin with additional salt and black pepper.

Pour the chicken or turkey broth into the bottom of the roasting pan.

Roast the turkey in the preheated oven for approximately 1.5 to 2 hours or until the internal temperature reaches 165°F (74°C) in the thickest part of the breast.

Baste the turkey with the pan juices every 30 minutes to keep it moist.

Once the turkey is cooked, remove it from the oven and let it rest for about 15-20 minutes before carving.

Carve the turkey breast and serve with the roasted vegetables and pan juices.

This Herb-Roasted Turkey Breast is a flavorful and succulent dish, perfect for a smaller gathering or when you prefer white meat. Enjoy your delicious herb-infused turkey!

Cauliflower Rice Pilaf

Ingredients:

- 1 medium-sized cauliflower head
- 2 tablespoons olive oil or butter
- 1 onion, finely chopped
- 2 cloves garlic, minced
- 1/2 cup carrots, finely diced
- 1/2 cup green peas (fresh or frozen)
- 1/4 cup chopped bell peppers (any color)
- 1/4 cup sliced almonds (optional, for garnish)
- 2 tablespoons fresh parsley, chopped (for garnish)
- Salt and black pepper to taste

Instructions:

Cut the cauliflower into florets and place them in a food processor. Pulse until the cauliflower resembles rice or couscous. Be careful not to over-process.

Heat olive oil or butter in a large skillet over medium heat.

Add chopped onions and sauté until they become translucent.

Add minced garlic to the onions and sauté for an additional 1-2 minutes until fragrant.

Stir in finely diced carrots, green peas, and chopped bell peppers. Cook for 3-4 minutes until the vegetables begin to soften.

Add the riced cauliflower to the skillet and stir to combine with the vegetables.

Season the cauliflower rice pilaf with salt and black pepper to taste. Continue to cook for another 5-7 minutes, stirring occasionally, until the cauliflower is tender but not mushy.

Optional: In a separate small pan, toast sliced almonds over medium heat until golden brown.

Garnish the cauliflower rice pilaf with toasted almonds and chopped fresh parsley.

Taste and adjust the seasoning if needed.

Serve the Cauliflower Rice Pilaf as a side dish or a light main course.

This Cauliflower Rice Pilaf is a low-carb and gluten-free alternative to traditional rice pilaf. It's versatile and can be customized with your favorite vegetables and herbs. Enjoy!

Caprese Salad with Balsamic Glaze

Ingredients:

- 4 large ripe tomatoes, sliced
- 8 ounces fresh mozzarella cheese, sliced
- Fresh basil leaves
- Extra-virgin olive oil
- Balsamic glaze or balsamic reduction
- Salt and black pepper to taste

Instructions:

Arrange the tomato slices and fresh mozzarella slices on a serving platter, alternating them for a visually appealing presentation.

Tuck fresh basil leaves between the tomato and mozzarella slices.

Drizzle extra-virgin olive oil over the tomato and mozzarella slices. Use a light hand, as you can always add more later.

Season the Caprese salad with salt and black pepper to taste.

Just before serving, generously drizzle balsamic glaze or balsamic reduction over the salad. The sweet and tangy balsamic adds depth and flavor to the dish.

Optionally, garnish with additional fresh basil leaves.

Serve the Caprese Salad with Balsamic as a refreshing appetizer or side dish.

This Caprese Salad with Balsamic is a classic Italian dish that celebrates the flavors of fresh tomatoes, mozzarella, and basil. It's simple, elegant, and perfect for showcasing the best of summer produce. Enjoy!

Lemon Basil Grilled Vegetables

Ingredients:

- Assorted vegetables, such as zucchini, bell peppers, cherry tomatoes, red onion, and mushrooms, washed and cut into bite-sized pieces
- 3 tablespoons olive oil
- Zest of 1 lemon
- Juice of 1 lemon
- 2 tablespoons fresh basil, chopped
- 2 cloves garlic, minced
- Salt and black pepper to taste

Instructions:

Preheat your grill to medium-high heat.

In a small bowl, whisk together olive oil, lemon zest, lemon juice, chopped fresh basil, minced garlic, salt, and black pepper to create the marinade.

Place the prepared vegetables in a large bowl.

Pour the marinade over the vegetables and toss until the vegetables are well-coated.

If using wooden skewers, soak them in water for about 20-30 minutes to prevent burning.

Thread the marinated vegetables onto skewers or place them directly on a grilling pan.

Grill the vegetables for about 10-15 minutes, turning occasionally, until they are tender and have nice grill marks.

Remove the grilled vegetables from the heat.

Optional: Drizzle any remaining marinade over the vegetables for extra flavor.

Serve the Lemon Basil Grilled Vegetables hot as a side dish or on their own.

This Lemon Basil Grilled Vegetables recipe adds a burst of fresh and citrusy flavors to your favorite veggies. It's a versatile dish that pairs well with various proteins or makes a great addition to salads or pasta. Enjoy!

Baked Tilapia with Lemon and Herbs

Ingredients:

- 4 tilapia fillets
- 2 tablespoons olive oil
- Zest of 1 lemon
- Juice of 1 lemon
- 2 cloves garlic, minced
- 1 teaspoon dried thyme
- 1 teaspoon dried rosemary
- 1 teaspoon dried oregano
- Salt and black pepper to taste
- Fresh parsley, chopped (for garnish)
- Lemon wedges (for serving)

Instructions:

Preheat your oven to 400°F (200°C).

In a small bowl, mix together olive oil, lemon zest, lemon juice, minced garlic, dried thyme, dried rosemary, dried oregano, salt, and black pepper.

Place the tilapia fillets in a baking dish, and brush the fillets with the lemon and herb mixture, ensuring they are well-coated.

If you prefer, you can let the tilapia marinate for about 15-30 minutes for more flavor.

Bake the tilapia in the preheated oven for about 12-15 minutes or until the fish flakes easily with a fork.

Optional: Broil the tilapia for an additional 2-3 minutes to get a golden brown crust on top.

Remove the baked tilapia from the oven and sprinkle chopped fresh parsley over the top.

Serve the Baked Tilapia with Lemon and Herbs hot, garnished with additional lemon wedges on the side.

This Baked Tilapia with Lemon and Herbs is a quick and healthy dish that's bursting with citrusy and herby flavors. It pairs well with a variety of side dishes like steamed vegetables, rice, or a light salad. Enjoy your delicious and nutritious meal!

Chickpea and Spinach Stew

Ingredients:

- 2 tablespoons olive oil
- 1 large onion, finely chopped
- 3 cloves garlic, minced
- 1 teaspoon ground cumin
- 1 teaspoon ground coriander
- 1 teaspoon smoked paprika
- 1/2 teaspoon ground turmeric
- 1/4 teaspoon cayenne pepper (adjust to taste)
- 1 can (15 ounces) chickpeas, drained and rinsed
- 1 can (14 ounces) diced tomatoes
- 1 cup vegetable broth
- 1 teaspoon tomato paste
- 1 bay leaf
- Salt and black pepper to taste
- 5 cups fresh spinach leaves, washed and chopped
- Juice of 1 lemon
- Fresh cilantro or parsley, chopped (for garnish)

Instructions:

In a large pot or Dutch oven, heat olive oil over medium heat.

Add chopped onions and sauté until they become soft and translucent.

Add minced garlic to the onions and sauté for an additional 1-2 minutes until fragrant.

Stir in ground cumin, ground coriander, smoked paprika, ground turmeric, and cayenne pepper. Cook for another minute to toast the spices.

Add chickpeas, diced tomatoes (with their juice), vegetable broth, tomato paste, bay leaf, salt, and black pepper to the pot. Stir to combine.

Bring the stew to a simmer, then reduce the heat to low. Cover and let it simmer for about 15-20 minutes, allowing the flavors to meld.

Add chopped fresh spinach to the pot and stir until the spinach wilts into the stew.

Squeeze the juice of one lemon into the stew and stir.

Taste and adjust the seasoning if needed.

Serve the Chickpea and Spinach Stew hot, garnished with fresh cilantro or parsley.

This Chickpea and Spinach Stew is a nutritious and flavorful dish that's easy to prepare. It's perfect on its own or served with rice, quinoa, or crusty bread. Enjoy!

Grilled Portobello Mushrooms

Ingredients:

- 4 large portobello mushrooms, stems removed
- 3 tablespoons balsamic vinegar
- 2 tablespoons olive oil
- 2 cloves garlic, minced
- 1 teaspoon dried thyme
- Salt and black pepper to taste
- Fresh parsley, chopped (for garnish)

Instructions:

Preheat your grill to medium-high heat.

In a small bowl, whisk together balsamic vinegar, olive oil, minced garlic, dried thyme, salt, and black pepper to create the marinade.

Clean the portobello mushrooms with a damp cloth to remove any dirt. Remove the stems.

Brush both sides of the mushrooms with the prepared marinade, ensuring they are well-coated.

Place the marinated mushrooms on the preheated grill, gill side down. Grill for about 5-7 minutes on each side, or until the mushrooms are tender and have nice grill marks.

Optional: Brush the mushrooms with additional marinade during grilling for extra flavor.

Once the mushrooms are cooked, remove them from the grill and place them on a serving plate.

Garnish the Grilled Portobello Mushrooms with fresh chopped parsley.

Serve hot as a side dish, on a salad, or as a burger alternative.

These Grilled Portobello Mushrooms are savory, smoky, and versatile. They can be enjoyed on their own or used in various dishes, such as sandwiches, salads, or as a side to complement your favorite grilled entrees. Enjoy!

Broccoli and Quinoa Casserole

Ingredients:

- 1 cup quinoa, rinsed and drained
- 2 cups broccoli florets
- 1 tablespoon olive oil
- 1 onion, finely chopped
- 2 cloves garlic, minced
- 1 red bell pepper, diced
- 1 carrot, grated
- 1/4 cup all-purpose flour or whole wheat flour
- 2 cups vegetable broth
- 2 cups milk (dairy or plant-based)
- 1 teaspoon Dijon mustard
- 1 teaspoon dried thyme
- Salt and black pepper to taste
- 2 cups shredded cheddar cheese (or a blend of your favorite cheeses)
- 1/2 cup grated Parmesan cheese
- Breadcrumbs (optional, for topping)
- Fresh parsley, chopped (for garnish)

Instructions:

Preheat your oven to 375°F (190°C). Grease a baking dish.

Cook quinoa according to package instructions. Set aside.

- Steam the broccoli florets until they are just tender. You can steam them on the stovetop or in the microwave.
- In a large skillet, heat olive oil over medium heat. Add chopped onions and sauté until they become soft and translucent.
- Add minced garlic, diced red bell pepper, and grated carrot to the skillet. Cook for an additional 3-4 minutes until the vegetables are softened.
- Sprinkle flour over the vegetables and stir to combine, creating a roux.
- Gradually whisk in vegetable broth and milk to the skillet, ensuring there are no lumps. Continue to stir until the mixture thickens.
- Stir in Dijon mustard, dried thyme, salt, and black pepper.
- Add shredded cheddar cheese and grated Parmesan cheese to the skillet. Stir until the cheeses are melted and the sauce is smooth.
- In a large mixing bowl, combine cooked quinoa, steamed broccoli, and the cheese sauce. Mix well to ensure even coating.
- Transfer the quinoa and broccoli mixture to the prepared baking dish.
- Optional: Sprinkle breadcrumbs over the top for a crunchy topping.
- Bake in the preheated oven for about 20-25 minutes, or until the casserole is heated through and bubbly.
- Remove from the oven and let it rest for a few minutes.
- Garnish with fresh chopped parsley before serving.

This Broccoli and Quinoa Casserole is a nutritious and comforting dish that combines the goodness of quinoa, broccoli, and cheesy goodness. It's perfect as a main dish or a satisfying side. Enjoy!

Greek Yogurt Chicken Salad

Ingredients:

- 2 cups cooked chicken breast, shredded or diced
- 1/2 cup Greek yogurt (plain)
- 1/4 cup mayonnaise
- 1 tablespoon Dijon mustard
- 1 celery stalk, finely chopped
- 1/4 cup red onion, finely chopped
- 1/4 cup cucumber, finely diced
- 1/4 cup cherry tomatoes, halved
- 1/4 cup Kalamata olives, pitted and sliced
- 1 tablespoon fresh dill, chopped
- 1 tablespoon fresh parsley, chopped
- Juice of 1 lemon
- Salt and black pepper to taste
- Lettuce leaves or whole-grain bread (for serving)

Instructions:

In a large mixing bowl, combine shredded or diced chicken breast, Greek yogurt, mayonnaise, and Dijon mustard. Mix well to coat the chicken evenly.

Add chopped celery, red onion, cucumber, cherry tomatoes, Kalamata olives, fresh dill, and fresh parsley to the bowl. Mix until all ingredients are well combined.

Squeeze the juice of one lemon over the chicken salad mixture.

Season the Greek Yogurt Chicken Salad with salt and black pepper to taste. Adjust the seasoning according to your preferences.

Refrigerate the chicken salad for at least 30 minutes to allow the flavors to meld.

Serve the Greek Yogurt Chicken Salad on a bed of lettuce leaves, in a sandwich, or with whole-grain bread.

This Greek Yogurt Chicken Salad is a lighter and healthier alternative to traditional chicken salad, thanks to the use of Greek yogurt. It's rich in flavors, packed with protein, and makes a satisfying meal or snack. Enjoy!

Lemon Rosemary Roasted Potatoes

Ingredients:

- 2 pounds (about 1 kg) baby potatoes, washed and halved
- 3 tablespoons olive oil
- Zest of 1 lemon
- Juice of 1 lemon
- 2 tablespoons fresh rosemary, chopped
- 3 cloves garlic, minced
- Salt and black pepper to taste
- Lemon slices (for garnish)
- Fresh parsley, chopped (for garnish)

Instructions:

Preheat your oven to 400°F (200°C).

In a large mixing bowl, combine halved baby potatoes with olive oil, lemon zest, lemon juice, chopped fresh rosemary, minced garlic, salt, and black pepper. Toss until the potatoes are well coated with the seasoning.

Spread the seasoned potatoes in a single layer on a baking sheet lined with parchment paper or lightly greased.

Roast the potatoes in the preheated oven for about 30-35 minutes, or until they are golden brown and crispy on the edges. Make sure to stir the potatoes halfway through the cooking time for even roasting.

Once the potatoes are done, remove them from the oven.

Garnish the Lemon Rosemary Roasted Potatoes with lemon slices and chopped fresh parsley.

Serve hot as a side dish to your favorite main course.

These Lemon Rosemary Roasted Potatoes are a flavorful and aromatic side dish that pairs well with a variety of meals. The combination of citrusy lemon, fragrant rosemary, and crispy potatoes is sure to be a hit. Enjoy!

Avocado and Black Bean Salad

Ingredients:

- 1 can (15 ounces) black beans, drained and rinsed
- 2 ripe avocados, diced
- 1 cup corn kernels (fresh, frozen, or canned)
- 1 cup cherry tomatoes, halved
- 1/2 red onion, finely chopped
- 1/4 cup fresh cilantro, chopped
- Juice of 2 limes
- 2 tablespoons olive oil
- 1 teaspoon ground cumin
- Salt and black pepper to taste
- Optional: Jalapeño, diced (for extra heat)
- Optional: Feta cheese, crumbled (for garnish)

Instructions:

In a large mixing bowl, combine black beans, diced avocados, corn kernels, cherry tomatoes, chopped red onion, and chopped cilantro.

In a small bowl, whisk together lime juice, olive oil, ground cumin, salt, and black pepper. Adjust the seasoning to taste.

Pour the dressing over the salad ingredients.

Toss the salad gently until all ingredients are well coated with the dressing.

Optional: Add diced jalapeño for extra heat if desired.

If you're adding feta cheese, crumble it over the top just before serving.

Refrigerate the Avocado and Black Bean Salad for at least 30 minutes to allow the flavors to meld.

Serve chilled as a refreshing side dish or a light meal.

This Avocado and Black Bean Salad is not only delicious but also loaded with healthy ingredients. It's a perfect option for a quick and nutritious lunch or as a side dish for picnics and barbecues. Enjoy!

Herb Crusted Baked Chicken

Ingredients:

- 4 boneless, skinless chicken breasts
- 2 tablespoons olive oil
- 2 teaspoons Dijon mustard
- 2 cloves garlic, minced
- 1 cup breadcrumbs (preferably whole wheat or panko)
- 2 tablespoons fresh parsley, chopped
- 1 tablespoon fresh thyme leaves, chopped
- 1 teaspoon dried oregano
- 1 teaspoon dried rosemary
- Salt and black pepper to taste
- Lemon wedges for serving (optional)

Instructions:

Preheat your oven to 400°F (200°C). Grease a baking dish or line it with parchment paper.

In a small bowl, mix together olive oil, Dijon mustard, and minced garlic.

In another bowl, combine breadcrumbs, chopped fresh parsley, chopped fresh thyme, dried oregano, dried rosemary, salt, and black pepper. Mix well to create the herb crust.

Pat the chicken breasts dry with paper towels.

Brush each chicken breast with the olive oil and Dijon mustard mixture.

Press each chicken breast into the herb crust mixture, coating both sides evenly. Press down to ensure the crust adheres to the chicken.

Place the herb-crusted chicken breasts in the prepared baking dish.

Bake in the preheated oven for about 20-25 minutes or until the chicken is cooked through and the crust is golden brown.

If you have a meat thermometer, the internal temperature of the chicken should reach 165°F (74°C).

Once done, remove the herb-crusted baked chicken from the oven and let it rest for a few minutes.

Serve the chicken with lemon wedges if desired.

This Herb-Crusted Baked Chicken is a tasty and healthier alternative to fried chicken. The combination of herbs adds wonderful flavor, and the baking method ensures a crispy crust without deep frying. Enjoy your delicious and herb-infused chicken!

Ratatouille with Herbs de Provence

Ingredients:

- 1 eggplant, diced
- 2 zucchinis, diced
- 1 red bell pepper, diced
- 1 yellow bell pepper, diced
- 1 onion, finely chopped
- 3 cloves garlic, minced
- 2 tomatoes, diced
- 1 can (14 ounces) crushed tomatoes
- 2 tablespoons tomato paste
- 2 teaspoons Herbes de Provence (a blend of dried herbs like thyme, rosemary, oregano, marjoram, and savory)
- Salt and black pepper to taste
- 3 tablespoons olive oil
- Fresh basil, chopped (for garnish)

Instructions:

Preheat your oven to 375°F (190°C).

In a large skillet, heat olive oil over medium heat.

Add chopped onions and garlic to the skillet, sautéing until the onions are soft and translucent.

Add diced eggplant, zucchini, red and yellow bell peppers to the skillet. Cook for about 5-7 minutes, or until the vegetables start to soften.

Stir in diced tomatoes, crushed tomatoes, and tomato paste. Mix well.

Season the mixture with Herbes de Provence, salt, and black pepper. Adjust the seasoning to taste.

Transfer the mixture to a baking dish, spreading it evenly.

Bake in the preheated oven for about 30-40 minutes, or until the vegetables are tender and the flavors have melded.

Remove from the oven and let it rest for a few minutes.

Garnish with fresh chopped basil before serving.

Serve Ratatouille with Herbes de Provence as a side dish, over rice, quinoa, or as a main course. This flavorful and aromatic dish is a celebration of summer vegetables and the herbs of Provence. Enjoy!

Shrimp and Zucchini Skewers

Ingredients:

- 1 pound large shrimp, peeled and deveined
- 2 zucchinis, sliced into rounds
- 1 lemon, sliced into wedges (for garnish)

Marinade:

- 3 tablespoons olive oil
- 2 cloves garlic, minced
- 1 teaspoon lemon zest
- 2 tablespoons fresh lemon juice
- 1 teaspoon dried oregano
- 1 teaspoon paprika
- Salt and black pepper to taste

Instructions:

In a bowl, whisk together all the ingredients for the marinade - olive oil, minced garlic, lemon zest, lemon juice, dried oregano, paprika, salt, and black pepper.

Pat the shrimp dry with paper towels and place them in a resealable plastic bag or a shallow dish.

Pour the marinade over the shrimp, ensuring they are well coated. Seal the bag or cover the dish and refrigerate for at least 30 minutes to marinate.

Preheat the grill to medium-high heat.

While the shrimp are marinating, prepare the zucchini rounds.

Thread the marinated shrimp and zucchini rounds onto skewers, alternating between shrimp and zucchini.

Grill the skewers for about 2-3 minutes per side, or until the shrimp are opaque and cooked through.

Remove the skewers from the grill and transfer them to a serving platter.

Optional: Squeeze fresh lemon juice over the skewers for an extra burst of flavor. Garnish with additional lemon wedges.

Serve the Shrimp and Zucchini Skewers hot as a delicious and light dish. These skewers are perfect for a quick and flavorful meal, especially during the warmer months. Enjoy!

Lemon Garlic Roasted Asparagus

Ingredients:

- 1 bunch fresh asparagus, tough ends trimmed
- 2 tablespoons olive oil
- 3 cloves garlic, minced
- Zest of 1 lemon
- Juice of 1 lemon
- Salt and black pepper to taste
- Grated Parmesan cheese (optional, for serving)
- Fresh parsley, chopped (for garnish)

Instructions:

Preheat your oven to 400°F (200°C).

Place the trimmed asparagus on a baking sheet.

In a small bowl, mix together olive oil, minced garlic, lemon zest, lemon juice, salt, and black pepper.

Drizzle the olive oil mixture over the asparagus and toss to coat evenly.

Arrange the asparagus in a single layer on the baking sheet.

Roast in the preheated oven for about 12-15 minutes, or until the asparagus is tender and slightly crispy at the tips.

Optional: Sprinkle grated Parmesan cheese over the roasted asparagus during the last 5 minutes of cooking for a cheesy finish.

Remove from the oven and transfer the roasted asparagus to a serving platter. Garnish with fresh chopped parsley.

Serve the Lemon Garlic Roasted Asparagus as a side dish, and enjoy!

This Lemon Garlic Roasted Asparagus is a quick and flavorful way to prepare this seasonal vegetable. The combination of zesty lemon and savory garlic enhances the natural taste of asparagus. It's a perfect side dish for any meal!

Baked Eggplant Parmesan

Ingredients:

- 2 large eggplants, peeled and sliced into 1/2-inch rounds
- Salt, for drawing out moisture
- 2 cups all-purpose flour (for dredging)
- 4 large eggs
- 2 tablespoons water
- 3 cups breadcrumbs (preferably Italian-style or panko)
- 1 cup grated Parmesan cheese
- Olive oil, for brushing the eggplant slices
- 4 cups marinara sauce (store-bought or homemade)
- 2 cups shredded mozzarella cheese
- Fresh basil or parsley, chopped (for garnish)

Instructions:

Preheat your oven to 375°F (190°C).

Place the eggplant slices on a paper towel-lined baking sheet. Sprinkle salt on both sides of each slice and let them sit for about 30 minutes to draw out excess moisture. Pat the eggplant slices dry with paper towels.

Set up a dredging station with three shallow dishes: one with flour, one with beaten eggs and water, and one with a mixture of breadcrumbs and grated Parmesan.

Dip each eggplant slice into the flour, shaking off excess. Next, dip it into the egg mixture, allowing any excess to drip off. Finally, coat it in the breadcrumb and Parmesan mixture, pressing the breadcrumbs onto the eggplant to adhere.

Place the breaded eggplant slices on a baking sheet lined with parchment paper. Brush each slice with olive oil on both sides.

Bake in the preheated oven for about 20-25 minutes or until the eggplant slices are golden brown and crispy.

In a baking dish, spread a thin layer of marinara sauce.

Arrange half of the baked eggplant slices in the baking dish, overlapping slightly.

Spoon more marinara sauce over the eggplant slices and sprinkle half of the shredded mozzarella cheese.

Repeat with another layer of the remaining eggplant slices, marinara sauce, and mozzarella.

Bake in the oven for an additional 25-30 minutes, or until the cheese is melted and bubbly.

Garnish with chopped fresh basil or parsley before serving.

Serve the Baked Eggplant Parmesan hot, and enjoy this delicious and comforting dish that's a healthier twist on the classic.

Herb-Marinated Grilled Tofu

Ingredients:

- 1 block of extra-firm tofu
- 2 tablespoons soy sauce
- 2 tablespoons olive oil
- 2 cloves garlic, minced
- 1 teaspoon dried oregano
- 1 teaspoon dried thyme
- 1 teaspoon dried rosemary
- 1/2 teaspoon black pepper
- 1 tablespoon lemon juice
- Optional: 1 tablespoon maple syrup or agave nectar for a touch of sweetness

Instructions:

Prepare the Tofu:
- Press the tofu to remove excess water. You can do this by wrapping the tofu block in a clean kitchen towel and placing something heavy on top (like a cast-iron skillet) for about 15-30 minutes.

Make the Marinade:
- In a bowl, whisk together soy sauce, olive oil, minced garlic, oregano, thyme, rosemary, black pepper, and lemon juice. If you prefer a slightly sweet flavor, you can add maple syrup or agave nectar.

Cut and Marinate the Tofu:
- Cut the pressed tofu into slices or cubes, depending on your preference.

- Place the tofu in a shallow dish or a resealable plastic bag.
- Pour the marinade over the tofu, making sure each piece is well-coated.
- Allow the tofu to marinate for at least 30 minutes to let the flavors absorb. For even better results, you can marinate it for several hours or overnight in the refrigerator.

Grill the Tofu:

- Preheat your grill to medium-high heat.
- If you're using skewers, thread the marinated tofu onto them.
- Grill the tofu for 5-7 minutes on each side, or until it has nice grill marks and is heated through.

Serve:

- Remove the tofu from the grill and let it rest for a couple of minutes.
- Serve the herb-marinated grilled tofu on its own or as part of a salad, sandwich, or bowl.

Feel free to customize the marinade with your favorite herbs and spices. This dish is not only tasty but also a great source of plant-based protein. Enjoy!

Tomato Basil Quinoa Pilaf

Ingredients:

- 1 cup quinoa, rinsed and drained
- 2 cups vegetable broth or water
- 1 tablespoon olive oil
- 1 onion, finely chopped
- 2 cloves garlic, minced
- 1 can (14 ounces) diced tomatoes (or use fresh tomatoes, diced)
- 1 teaspoon dried basil (or 2 tablespoons fresh basil, chopped)
- Salt and pepper to taste
- Optional: Grated Parmesan cheese for serving

Instructions:

Rinse the Quinoa:

- Rinse the quinoa under cold water using a fine-mesh sieve. This helps remove any bitter coating.

Cook the Quinoa:

- In a medium saucepan, bring the vegetable broth or water to a boil.
- Add the rinsed quinoa, reduce the heat to low, cover, and simmer for about 15 minutes or until the quinoa is cooked and the liquid is absorbed.
- Once cooked, fluff the quinoa with a fork and set aside.

Sauté Onion and Garlic:

- In a large skillet or pan, heat olive oil over medium heat.
- Add chopped onion and sauté until it becomes translucent.

- Add minced garlic and sauté for an additional 1-2 minutes until fragrant.

Combine with Tomatoes and Basil:

- Add diced tomatoes (with their juices) to the skillet.
- Stir in dried basil or fresh chopped basil.
- Allow the mixture to simmer for 5-7 minutes, letting the flavors meld.

Combine Quinoa and Tomato Mixture:

- Add the cooked quinoa to the tomato mixture in the skillet.
- Stir well to combine, ensuring the quinoa is evenly coated with the tomato and basil mixture.

Season and Serve:

- Season with salt and pepper to taste.
- Optionally, sprinkle with grated Parmesan cheese before serving.

Serve Warm:

- Serve the Tomato Basil Quinoa Pilaf warm as a side dish or as a light main course.

This Tomato Basil Quinoa Pilaf is a versatile dish that pairs well with grilled vegetables, roasted chicken, or as a standalone vegetarian option. Enjoy your delicious and nutritious meal!

Orange Glazed Grilled Chicken

Ingredients:

- 4 boneless, skinless chicken breasts
- Salt and pepper to taste
- 1 tablespoon olive oil (for brushing the grill)

For the Orange Glaze:

- 1 cup orange juice (freshly squeezed is preferred)
- Zest of one orange
- 1/4 cup soy sauce
- 2 tablespoons honey
- 1 tablespoon Dijon mustard
- 2 cloves garlic, minced
- 1 teaspoon grated ginger
- 1/4 teaspoon red pepper flakes (optional, for some heat)
- 1 tablespoon cornstarch (optional, for thickening)

Instructions:

Preheat the Grill:
- Preheat your grill to medium-high heat.

Prepare the Chicken:
- Season the chicken breasts with salt and pepper on both sides.

Make the Orange Glaze:

- In a small saucepan, combine orange juice, orange zest, soy sauce, honey, Dijon mustard, minced garlic, grated ginger, and red pepper flakes (if using).
- Bring the mixture to a simmer over medium heat and let it cook for about 5-7 minutes, allowing it to reduce slightly.
- If you prefer a thicker glaze, mix 1 tablespoon of cornstarch with a little water to create a slurry. Stir this into the glaze and continue to cook until it thickens.

Grill the Chicken:

- Brush the grill grates with olive oil to prevent sticking.
- Place the seasoned chicken breasts on the preheated grill and cook for about 6-8 minutes per side or until the internal temperature reaches 165°F (74°C).

Glaze the Chicken:

- Brush the orange glaze onto the chicken during the last few minutes of grilling, allowing it to caramelize and impart flavor.

Serve:

- Once the chicken is cooked through and has a nice glaze, remove it from the grill.
- Let the chicken rest for a few minutes before serving.

Optional: Garnish and Enjoy:

- Garnish the grilled chicken with additional orange zest or chopped fresh herbs, such as parsley or cilantro, for a burst of freshness.

Serve the Orange Glazed Grilled Chicken with your favorite sides, such as rice, quinoa, or grilled vegetables. This dish is perfect for a summer barbecue or any time you want a delicious and citrusy grilled chicken. Enjoy!

Cabbage and Apple Slaw

Ingredients:

- 4 cups shredded green cabbage
- 2 cups shredded red cabbage
- 2 apples, cored and thinly sliced (use a sweet variety like Fuji or Honeycrisp)
- 1/2 cup thinly sliced red onion
- 1/2 cup chopped fresh cilantro or parsley (optional, for garnish)

For the Dressing:

- 1/3 cup mayonnaise
- 2 tablespoons apple cider vinegar
- 1 tablespoon Dijon mustard
- 2 tablespoons honey or maple syrup
- Salt and pepper to taste

Instructions:

Prepare the Vegetables:
- In a large bowl, combine the shredded green cabbage, shredded red cabbage, sliced apples, and thinly sliced red onion.

Make the Dressing:
- In a small bowl, whisk together the mayonnaise, apple cider vinegar, Dijon mustard, honey or maple syrup, salt, and pepper until well combined.

Combine and Toss:
- Pour the dressing over the cabbage and apple mixture.

- Toss everything together until the vegetables and apples are evenly coated with the dressing.

Chill:

- Cover the bowl and refrigerate the slaw for at least 30 minutes to allow the flavors to meld and the slaw to chill.

Garnish and Serve:

- Before serving, garnish the slaw with chopped cilantro or parsley if desired.

Adjust Seasoning:

- Taste the slaw and adjust the seasoning, adding more salt, pepper, or honey/maple syrup if needed.

Serve Cold:

- Serve the Cabbage and Apple Slaw cold as a refreshing side dish.

This slaw is a great accompaniment to grilled meats, sandwiches, tacos, or as a topping for pulled pork or fish tacos. It's versatile, colorful, and adds a delightful crunch to your meal. Enjoy!

Roasted Garlic Hummus

Ingredients:

- 1 can (15 ounces) chickpeas (garbanzo beans), drained and rinsed
- 1/3 cup tahini
- 3 tablespoons extra-virgin olive oil, plus extra for drizzling
- 1 whole head of garlic
- 1 teaspoon ground cumin
- 1/2 teaspoon smoked paprika (optional)
- Juice of 1 lemon
- Salt and pepper to taste
- 2 to 4 tablespoons water (for adjusting consistency)
- Fresh parsley, chopped, for garnish (optional)

Instructions:

Roast the Garlic:
- Preheat the oven to 400°F (200°C).
- Peel away most of the outer layers of the garlic bulb, leaving the individual cloves connected.
- Cut off the top of the bulb to expose the cloves.
- Place the garlic bulb on a piece of aluminum foil, drizzle with olive oil, and wrap it tightly in the foil.
- Roast in the preheated oven for about 30-40 minutes or until the garlic cloves are soft and golden brown.
- Allow the roasted garlic to cool slightly before handling.

Prepare Chickpeas:
- In a food processor, combine the drained chickpeas, tahini, olive oil, cumin, and smoked paprika (if using).

Squeeze Roasted Garlic:
- Squeeze the roasted garlic cloves out of their skins into the food processor.

Add Lemon Juice and Blend:
- Add the lemon juice to the food processor.
- Process the mixture until smooth, stopping to scrape down the sides as needed.

Adjust Consistency:
- With the food processor running, slowly add water, one tablespoon at a time, until you reach your desired consistency.

Season:
- Season the hummus with salt and pepper to taste. Adjust the seasoning as needed.

Serve:
- Transfer the hummus to a serving bowl.
- Drizzle with a bit of olive oil and garnish with chopped fresh parsley if desired.

Optional: Customize:
- Feel free to customize the hummus with additional toppings like pine nuts, a sprinkle of paprika, or a drizzle of balsamic glaze.

Serve the Roasted Garlic Hummus with pita bread, fresh vegetables, or as a spread on sandwiches. It's a delicious and healthy option for any occasion. Enjoy!

Herb-Rubbed Pork Tenderloin

Ingredients:

- 2 pork tenderloins (about 1 to 1.5 pounds each)
- 2 tablespoons olive oil
- 3 cloves garlic, minced
- 1 tablespoon fresh rosemary, finely chopped
- 1 tablespoon fresh thyme, finely chopped
- 1 tablespoon fresh sage, finely chopped
- 1 teaspoon dried oregano
- 1 teaspoon dried basil
- 1 teaspoon salt
- 1/2 teaspoon black pepper

Instructions:

Preheat the Oven:

- Preheat your oven to 400°F (200°C).

Prepare the Pork Tenderloins:

- Trim any excess fat or silver skin from the pork tenderloins.
- Pat the pork tenderloins dry with paper towels.

Make the Herb Rub:

- In a small bowl, combine the minced garlic, chopped rosemary, thyme, sage, dried oregano, dried basil, salt, black pepper, and olive oil. Mix well to form a paste.

Rub the Pork Tenderloins:

- Rub the herb mixture all over the pork tenderloins, ensuring that they are evenly coated.

Sear the Pork:

- Heat an oven-safe skillet over medium-high heat.
- Add a bit of olive oil to the skillet.
- Sear the pork tenderloins on all sides until they develop a nice golden-brown crust.

Transfer to Oven:

- Place the skillet with the seared pork tenderloins into the preheated oven.

Roast in the Oven:

- Roast the pork tenderloins in the oven for about 15-20 minutes or until the internal temperature reaches 145°F (63°C). Cooking time may vary based on the size of your tenderloins.

Rest and Slice:

- Once done, remove the pork from the oven and let it rest for 5-10 minutes before slicing. This allows the juices to redistribute.

Serve:

- Slice the pork tenderloins into medallions and serve with your favorite side dishes.

Optional: Pan Sauce (Gravy):

- If desired, you can make a simple pan sauce by deglazing the skillet with a bit of chicken broth or white wine after removing the pork from the oven. Reduce the liquid, season to taste, and drizzle over the sliced pork.

This herb-rubbed pork tenderloin is a delicious and elegant dish that works well for both casual dinners and special occasions. Enjoy!

Lemon Cilantro Quinoa

Ingredients:

- 1 cup quinoa, rinsed and drained
- 2 cups vegetable broth or water
- Zest of 1 lemon
- Juice of 1 lemon
- 1/4 cup fresh cilantro, chopped
- 2 tablespoons olive oil
- Salt and pepper to taste

Instructions:

Cook the Quinoa:
- In a medium saucepan, bring the vegetable broth or water to a boil.
- Add the rinsed quinoa, reduce the heat to low, cover, and simmer for about 15 minutes or until the quinoa is cooked and the liquid is absorbed.
- Fluff the quinoa with a fork and allow it to cool slightly.

Prepare Lemon Zest and Juice:
- While the quinoa is cooking, zest the lemon and squeeze out the juice.

Combine Ingredients:
- In a large bowl, combine the cooked quinoa, lemon zest, lemon juice, chopped cilantro, and olive oil.
- Toss the ingredients together until well combined.

Season:

- Season the lemon cilantro quinoa with salt and pepper to taste. Adjust the seasoning as needed.

Serve:

- Serve the Lemon Cilantro Quinoa as a side dish with grilled chicken, fish, or roasted vegetables.

Optional Additions:

- You can customize the dish by adding extras like chopped cherry tomatoes, diced cucumber, or crumbled feta cheese for additional flavor and texture.

Chill (Optional):

- If you prefer a cold or room temperature quinoa salad, refrigerate the dish for at least 30 minutes before serving.

This Lemon Cilantro Quinoa is not only delicious but also a great source of protein and fiber. It's perfect for light and healthy meals, and the bright flavors make it a wonderful addition to your menu. Enjoy!

Grilled Vegetable Wrap

Ingredients:

For Grilled Vegetables:

- 1 zucchini, sliced lengthwise
- 1 yellow squash, sliced lengthwise
- 1 bell pepper (red, yellow, or green), sliced into strips
- 1 red onion, sliced into rings
- 1 eggplant, sliced into rounds
- 2 tablespoons olive oil
- Salt and pepper to taste
- 1 teaspoon dried oregano or Italian seasoning (optional)

For the Dressing:

- 3 tablespoons balsamic vinegar
- 2 tablespoons olive oil
- 1 clove garlic, minced
- 1 teaspoon Dijon mustard
- Salt and pepper to taste

Additional Wrap Ingredients:

- Whole-grain or your favorite tortillas/wraps
- Fresh greens (lettuce, spinach, arugula, etc.)
- Hummus or tzatziki (optional)

- Feta cheese or goat cheese, crumbled (optional)

Instructions:

Preheat the Grill:
- Preheat your grill or grill pan over medium-high heat.

Prepare Vegetables:
- In a large bowl, toss the sliced zucchini, yellow squash, bell pepper, red onion, and eggplant with olive oil, salt, pepper, and dried oregano or Italian seasoning if using.

Grill Vegetables:
- Grill the vegetables until they have nice grill marks and are tender. The cooking time will vary for each vegetable, but generally, it takes about 5-8 minutes per side.

Make the Dressing:
- In a small bowl, whisk together balsamic vinegar, olive oil, minced garlic, Dijon mustard, salt, and pepper to create the dressing.

Assemble the Wraps:
- Lay out the tortillas or wraps on a clean surface.
- Spread a layer of hummus or tzatziki on each wrap if using.
- Place a handful of fresh greens on each wrap.

Add Grilled Vegetables:
- Arrange the grilled vegetables on top of the greens.

Drizzle with Dressing:
- Drizzle the balsamic dressing over the grilled vegetables.

Optional Toppings:

- If desired, sprinkle crumbled feta cheese or goat cheese over the vegetables.

Wrap it Up:

- Fold the sides of the tortilla inwards and then roll it up tightly, creating a wrap.

Serve:

- Slice the wraps in half diagonally and serve immediately.

This Grilled Vegetable Wrap is a versatile and satisfying dish, perfect for lunch or dinner. Feel free to customize it with your favorite vegetables, sauces, or cheeses. Enjoy!

White Bean and Vegetable Soup

Ingredients:

- 1 cup dried white beans (such as navy beans), soaked overnight or quick-soaked
- 2 tablespoons olive oil
- 1 onion, finely chopped
- 2 carrots, diced
- 2 celery stalks, diced
- 3 cloves garlic, minced
- 1 teaspoon dried thyme
- 1 teaspoon dried rosemary
- 1 bay leaf
- 6 cups vegetable broth
- 1 can (14 ounces) diced tomatoes, undrained
- 2 zucchini, diced
- 1 cup green beans, trimmed and cut into bite-sized pieces
- Salt and pepper to taste
- Fresh parsley, chopped (for garnish)

Instructions:

Prepare the White Beans:
- If you haven't done a quick soak, drain and rinse the soaked white beans.

Sauté Vegetables:
- In a large soup pot, heat olive oil over medium heat.

- Add chopped onion, carrots, and celery. Sauté until the vegetables are softened, about 5-7 minutes.

Add Garlic and Herbs:

- Add minced garlic, dried thyme, dried rosemary, and bay leaf. Sauté for an additional 1-2 minutes until fragrant.

Add Broth and Tomatoes:

- Pour in the vegetable broth and add the diced tomatoes with their juices. Stir to combine.

Add White Beans:

- Add the soaked and drained white beans to the pot.

Simmer:

- Bring the soup to a boil, then reduce the heat to low and let it simmer for about 30 minutes, or until the beans are tender.

Add Zucchini and Green Beans:

- Add the diced zucchini and green beans to the soup. Simmer for an additional 10-15 minutes or until the vegetables are tender.

Season:

- Season the soup with salt and pepper to taste. Adjust the seasoning as needed.

Garnish and Serve:

- Remove the bay leaf.
- Ladle the soup into bowls and garnish with chopped fresh parsley.

Serve Warm:

- Serve the White Bean and Vegetable Soup warm, optionally with a side of crusty bread.

Feel free to customize the soup with additional vegetables, such as spinach or kale, and adjust the herbs and seasonings to suit your taste. This soup is not only delicious but also a great source of fiber and protein. Enjoy!

Garlic and Herb Baked Cod

Ingredients:

- 4 cod fillets (about 6 ounces each)
- 3 tablespoons olive oil
- 4 cloves garlic, minced
- 1 tablespoon fresh parsley, chopped
- 1 teaspoon dried oregano
- 1 teaspoon dried thyme
- 1 teaspoon paprika
- Salt and pepper to taste
- Lemon wedges for serving

Instructions:

Preheat the Oven:

- Preheat your oven to 400°F (200°C).

Prepare the Cod:

- Pat the cod fillets dry with paper towels and place them in a baking dish or on a baking sheet lined with parchment paper.

Make the Herb Mixture:

- In a small bowl, combine the olive oil, minced garlic, chopped parsley, dried oregano, dried thyme, paprika, salt, and pepper. Mix well to create the herb mixture.

Coat the Cod:

- Brush the herb mixture over the top of each cod fillet, ensuring that they are evenly coated.

Bake the Cod:

- Bake in the preheated oven for about 12-15 minutes or until the cod flakes easily with a fork and is opaque in the center.

Optional Broil (for Crispy Top):

- If you like a slightly crispy top, you can broil the cod for an additional 1-2 minutes after baking, watching closely to avoid burning.

Serve:

- Remove the baked cod from the oven and squeeze fresh lemon juice over each fillet before serving.

Garnish:

- Garnish with additional chopped parsley if desired.

Serve Hot:

- Serve the Garlic and Herb Baked Cod hot, with your favorite sides such as steamed vegetables, rice, or a salad.

This recipe is not only delicious but also healthy and low in calories. The garlic and herb seasoning adds wonderful flavor to the mild taste of cod. Enjoy your tasty and nutritious meal!

Mediterranean Stuffed Bell Peppers

Ingredients:

- 4 large bell peppers (any color)
- 1 cup quinoa, cooked according to package instructions
- 1 can (15 ounces) chickpeas, drained and rinsed
- 1 cup cherry tomatoes, halved
- 1 cucumber, diced
- 1/2 red onion, finely chopped
- 1/2 cup Kalamata olives, pitted and chopped
- 1/2 cup crumbled feta cheese
- 1/4 cup fresh parsley, chopped
- 2 tablespoons fresh mint, chopped
- 3 tablespoons extra-virgin olive oil
- 2 tablespoons red wine vinegar
- 1 teaspoon dried oregano
- Salt and pepper to taste
- Lemon wedges for serving

Instructions:

Preheat the Oven:
- Preheat your oven to 375°F (190°C).

Prepare Bell Peppers:
- Cut the tops off the bell peppers, remove the seeds, and lightly brush the outside with olive oil.

- Place the peppers in a baking dish.

Prepare Quinoa:

- Cook the quinoa according to the package instructions and set aside.

Prepare the Filling:

- In a large bowl, combine the cooked quinoa, chickpeas, cherry tomatoes, cucumber, red onion, Kalamata olives, feta cheese, parsley, and mint.

Make the Dressing:

- In a small bowl, whisk together the olive oil, red wine vinegar, dried oregano, salt, and pepper.

Combine and Fill Peppers:

- Pour the dressing over the quinoa mixture and toss until everything is well coated.
- Spoon the quinoa mixture into the prepared bell peppers, pressing down gently to pack the filling.

Bake:

- Place the stuffed bell peppers in the preheated oven and bake for about 25-30 minutes or until the peppers are tender.

Serve:

- Remove the stuffed peppers from the oven and let them cool for a few minutes.
- Serve the Mediterranean Stuffed Bell Peppers with a squeeze of fresh lemon juice and additional chopped herbs if desired.

These stuffed peppers are not only colorful and visually appealing but also packed with a variety of textures and flavors. They make a satisfying and healthy main dish or a delightful side for your Mediterranean-inspired meals. Enjoy!

Lemon Dill Salmon Burgers

Ingredients:

For the Salmon Patties:

- 1 pound fresh salmon fillet, skin removed
- 1/2 cup breadcrumbs (panko or regular)
- 1/4 cup finely chopped red onion
- 2 tablespoons fresh dill, chopped
- Zest of 1 lemon
- 1 tablespoon Dijon mustard
- 1 large egg
- Salt and pepper to taste
- Olive oil for cooking

For the Lemon Dill Sauce:

- 1/2 cup mayonnaise
- 1 tablespoon Dijon mustard
- 1 tablespoon fresh dill, chopped
- 1 tablespoon lemon juice
- Salt and pepper to taste

For Serving:

- Burger buns
- Lettuce

- Tomato slices
- Red onion slices
- Avocado slices (optional)

Instructions:

Prepare Salmon Patties:

- Cut the fresh salmon into small chunks.
- In a food processor, pulse the salmon until it reaches a coarse, ground consistency. Be careful not to over-process; you want some texture.
- In a large bowl, combine the processed salmon, breadcrumbs, chopped red onion, fresh dill, lemon zest, Dijon mustard, egg, salt, and pepper.
- Mix until well combined.

Form Salmon Patties:

- Divide the mixture into 4 equal portions and shape each into a patty.

Cook Salmon Patties:

- Heat olive oil in a skillet over medium-high heat.
- Cook the salmon patties for about 4-5 minutes per side, or until they are golden brown and cooked through.

Make Lemon Dill Sauce:

- While the patties are cooking, prepare the lemon dill sauce. In a small bowl, whisk together mayonnaise, Dijon mustard, chopped dill, lemon juice, salt, and pepper.

Assemble Burgers:

- Toast the burger buns if desired.

- Spread a generous amount of lemon dill sauce on the bottom half of each bun.
- Place a salmon patty on each bun.
- Top with lettuce, tomato slices, red onion slices, and avocado if using.
- Place the top half of the bun on each burger.

Serve:

- Serve the Lemon Dill Salmon Burgers immediately, accompanied by your favorite side dishes.

These salmon burgers are light, flavorful, and perfect for a healthy meal. Feel free to customize the toppings to suit your preferences, and enjoy the fresh and zesty flavors of lemon and dill!

Roasted Butternut Squash Soup

Ingredients:

- 1 medium-sized butternut squash, peeled, seeded, and diced
- 1 large onion, chopped
- 2 carrots, peeled and chopped
- 2 cloves garlic, minced
- 2 tablespoons olive oil
- 1 teaspoon ground cinnamon
- 1/2 teaspoon ground nutmeg
- 1/4 teaspoon ground ginger
- Salt and black pepper to taste
- 4 cups vegetable broth (or chicken broth for a non-vegetarian version)
- 1 cup coconut milk or heavy cream (optional, for creaminess)
- Chopped fresh parsley or chives for garnish (optional)

Instructions:

Preheat the Oven:

- Preheat your oven to 400°F (200°C).

Prepare Vegetables:

- Place the diced butternut squash, chopped onion, and carrots on a baking sheet.
- Drizzle with olive oil, sprinkle with minced garlic, ground cinnamon, nutmeg, ground ginger, salt, and black pepper.
- Toss the vegetables to coat them evenly with the spices and oil.

Roast the Vegetables:

- Roast the vegetables in the preheated oven for about 30-40 minutes or until they are tender and have developed a golden color.

Blend the Soup:

- Transfer the roasted vegetables to a blender or food processor.
- Add the vegetable or chicken broth.
- Blend until smooth. You may need to do this in batches.

Heat the Soup:

- Pour the blended mixture into a pot and heat over medium heat.
- Stir in coconut milk or heavy cream if using, and adjust the consistency with more broth if needed.

Season:

- Taste the soup and adjust the seasoning with more salt and pepper if necessary.

Serve:

- Ladle the soup into bowls.
- Garnish with chopped fresh parsley or chives if desired.

Optional: Drizzle with Cream:

- If you'd like, you can drizzle a little extra coconut milk or cream over each serving before serving.

Enjoy this Roasted Butternut Squash Soup as a comforting appetizer or a light meal. Serve it with a side of crusty bread for a perfect winter treat!

Rosemary Roasted Chicken Thighs

Ingredients:

- 4 bone-in, skin-on chicken thighs
- 2 tablespoons olive oil
- 1 tablespoon fresh rosemary, chopped
- 2 cloves garlic, minced
- 1 teaspoon lemon zest
- 1 tablespoon lemon juice
- 1 teaspoon salt (adjust to taste)
- 1/2 teaspoon black pepper
- 1/2 teaspoon paprika
- Optional: 1 tablespoon honey for a touch of sweetness

Instructions:

Preheat your oven to 400°F (200°C).

In a small bowl, mix together the olive oil, chopped rosemary, minced garlic, lemon zest, lemon juice, salt, pepper, and paprika. If you like a touch of sweetness, you can add honey to the mixture as well.

Pat the chicken thighs dry with paper towels. This helps the skin crisp up during roasting.

Place the chicken thighs in a bowl or on a plate and brush the rosemary mixture over the chicken, making sure to coat both sides. You can use a brush or your hands to rub the mixture onto the chicken.

Place the chicken thighs, skin side up, on a baking sheet lined with parchment paper or aluminum foil. Arrange them with some space in between to allow for even cooking.

Roast the chicken in the preheated oven for about 35-40 minutes or until the internal temperature reaches 165°F (74°C) and the skin is golden and crispy.

Optional: For the last 5 minutes of cooking, you can switch the oven to broil to get an extra crispy finish on the skin.

Once the chicken is done, remove it from the oven and let it rest for a few minutes before serving.

Garnish with additional fresh rosemary or a slice of lemon if desired.

Serve these delicious rosemary roasted chicken thighs with your favorite side dishes, such as roasted vegetables, mashed potatoes, or a simple salad. Enjoy!

Quinoa and Black Bean Stuffed Peppers

Ingredients:

- 4 large bell peppers, any color
- 1 cup quinoa, rinsed and cooked according to package instructions
- 1 can (15 oz) black beans, drained and rinsed
- 1 cup corn kernels (fresh, frozen, or canned)
- 1 cup diced tomatoes
- 1 cup shredded cheese (cheddar, Monterey Jack, or a Mexican blend)
- 1/2 cup diced red onion
- 1/2 cup chopped fresh cilantro
- 1 teaspoon ground cumin
- 1 teaspoon chili powder
- 1/2 teaspoon garlic powder
- Salt and pepper to taste
- 2 tablespoons olive oil
- Optional toppings: sour cream, salsa, avocado slices

Instructions:

Preheat your oven to 375°F (190°C).

Cut the tops off the bell peppers, remove the seeds, and rinse them. If needed, trim the bottoms slightly to help them stand upright in the baking dish.

In a large mixing bowl, combine the cooked quinoa, black beans, corn, diced tomatoes, shredded cheese, red onion, cilantro, ground cumin, chili powder, garlic powder, salt, and pepper. Mix well to combine.

Drizzle the olive oil over the outside of the bell peppers and rub to coat. This helps them to roast nicely in the oven.

Stuff each bell pepper with the quinoa and black bean mixture, pressing it down gently to pack it.

Place the stuffed peppers in a baking dish and cover with aluminum foil.

Bake in the preheated oven for 25-30 minutes or until the peppers are tender.

Remove the foil and bake for an additional 5-10 minutes, allowing the cheese on top to melt and get slightly golden.

Once done, remove the stuffed peppers from the oven and let them cool for a few minutes.

Serve the quinoa and black bean stuffed peppers with your favorite toppings, such as sour cream, salsa, or avocado slices.

These stuffed peppers make for a delicious and nutritious meal. Enjoy!

Grilled Zucchini and Tomato Salad

Ingredients:

- 3 medium zucchini, sliced lengthwise
- 2 cups cherry tomatoes, halved
- 2 tablespoons olive oil
- 1 tablespoon balsamic vinegar
- 2 cloves garlic, minced
- Salt and pepper to taste
- 1/4 cup fresh basil, chopped
- 1/4 cup feta cheese, crumbled (optional)
- 1/4 cup pine nuts, toasted (optional)

Instructions:

Preheat your grill or grill pan to medium-high heat.

In a bowl, toss the zucchini slices with 1 tablespoon of olive oil, minced garlic, salt, and pepper.

Grill the zucchini slices for 2-3 minutes on each side or until they have nice grill marks and are tender but not mushy. Remove from the grill and let them cool slightly.

In a large mixing bowl, combine the grilled zucchini slices and cherry tomatoes.

In a small bowl, whisk together the remaining 1 tablespoon of olive oil and balsamic vinegar. Season with additional salt and pepper to taste.

Drizzle the dressing over the grilled zucchini and tomatoes, tossing gently to coat.

Sprinkle chopped fresh basil over the salad and toss again.

Optional: Top the salad with crumbled feta cheese and toasted pine nuts for added flavor and texture.

Serve the Grilled Zucchini and Tomato Salad immediately as a side dish or a light main course.

This salad is a delightful way to enjoy the flavors of grilled vegetables, and it's perfect for a summer meal. Enjoy!

Baked Herb-Crusted Whitefish

Ingredients:

- 4 whitefish fillets (such as cod, tilapia, or haddock)
- 1/2 cup breadcrumbs (panko or regular)
- 2 tablespoons fresh parsley, finely chopped
- 1 tablespoon fresh dill, finely chopped
- 1 tablespoon fresh chives, finely chopped
- 1 teaspoon dried oregano
- 1 teaspoon dried thyme
- 1/2 teaspoon garlic powder
- 1/2 teaspoon onion powder
- Salt and pepper to taste
- 1/4 cup melted butter or olive oil
- Lemon wedges for serving

Instructions:

Preheat your oven to 400°F (200°C). Line a baking sheet with parchment paper or lightly grease it.

In a shallow dish, combine breadcrumbs, chopped parsley, chopped dill, chopped chives, dried oregano, dried thyme, garlic powder, onion powder, salt, and pepper. Mix well to create the herb crust mixture.

Pat the whitefish fillets dry with paper towels.

Brush each fillet with melted butter or olive oil on both sides.

Press each fillet into the herb crust mixture, ensuring that the herbs and breadcrumbs adhere to the fish.

Place the coated fillets on the prepared baking sheet.

Bake in the preheated oven for 12-15 minutes or until the fish flakes easily with a fork and the crust is golden brown.

Optional: Broil for an additional 1-2 minutes at the end to achieve a crispier crust.

Remove the baked herb-crusted whitefish from the oven and let it rest for a couple of minutes.

Serve the whitefish fillets with lemon wedges on the side for squeezing over the top.

This herb-crusted whitefish recipe is light, flavorful, and pairs well with a variety of side dishes like roasted vegetables, quinoa, or a fresh green salad. Enjoy your meal!

Spinach and Mushroom Frittata

Ingredients:

- 8 large eggs
- 1/2 cup milk
- Salt and pepper to taste
- 2 tablespoons olive oil
- 1 small onion, finely chopped
- 8 oz (about 225g) mushrooms, sliced
- 2 cups fresh spinach, chopped
- 1/2 cup shredded cheese (cheddar, feta, or your choice)
- 1 teaspoon dried oregano or Italian seasoning (optional)
- 1/4 cup grated Parmesan cheese (optional)
- Fresh herbs (such as parsley or chives) for garnish (optional)

Instructions:

Preheat your oven to 375°F (190°C).

In a bowl, whisk together the eggs, milk, salt, and pepper until well combined. Set aside.

In an oven-safe skillet, heat olive oil over medium heat. Add chopped onions and sauté until softened, about 2-3 minutes.

Add sliced mushrooms to the skillet and cook until they release their moisture and become golden brown, about 5-6 minutes.

Add chopped spinach to the skillet and cook until wilted, about 2 minutes.

Pour the whisked egg mixture over the vegetables in the skillet. Allow it to cook on the stove for 2-3 minutes, lifting the edges with a spatula to let the uncooked eggs flow underneath.

Sprinkle shredded cheese evenly over the frittata and add dried oregano or Italian seasoning if desired.

Transfer the skillet to the preheated oven and bake for 12-15 minutes or until the frittata is set in the center and the edges are golden brown.

Optional: Sprinkle grated Parmesan cheese over the top during the last 5 minutes of baking for an extra layer of flavor.

Once done, remove the frittata from the oven and let it cool for a few minutes. Garnish with fresh herbs if desired, then slice and serve.

Enjoy your Spinach and Mushroom Frittata for breakfast, brunch, or a light dinner! It's versatile and can be customized with your favorite herbs and cheeses.

Lemon Garlic Shrimp Stir-Fry

Ingredients:

- 1 pound (about 450g) large shrimp, peeled and deveined
- 3 tablespoons soy sauce
- 2 tablespoons fresh lemon juice
- 1 tablespoon honey or maple syrup
- 3 cloves garlic, minced
- 1 teaspoon grated fresh ginger
- 1 teaspoon cornstarch
- 2 tablespoons vegetable oil, divided
- 1 red bell pepper, thinly sliced
- 1 yellow bell pepper, thinly sliced
- 1 cup snap peas, ends trimmed
- 1 medium carrot, julienned
- 4 green onions, sliced
- Sesame seeds for garnish (optional)
- Cooked rice or noodles for serving

Instructions:

In a bowl, whisk together soy sauce, fresh lemon juice, honey (or maple syrup), minced garlic, grated ginger, and cornstarch. This will be the marinade and sauce for the shrimp stir-fry.

Place the peeled and deveined shrimp in a shallow dish and pour half of the marinade over them. Toss to coat evenly and let them marinate for about 15-20 minutes.

In a large wok or skillet, heat 1 tablespoon of vegetable oil over medium-high heat.

Add the marinated shrimp to the hot wok and stir-fry for 2-3 minutes or until they turn pink and opaque. Remove the shrimp from the wok and set aside.

In the same wok, add another tablespoon of oil. Add the sliced red and yellow bell peppers, snap peas, and julienned carrot. Stir-fry for 3-4 minutes or until the vegetables are crisp-tender.

Return the cooked shrimp to the wok with the vegetables.

Pour the remaining marinade over the shrimp and vegetables. Stir-fry for an additional 2 minutes, allowing the sauce to thicken and coat everything.

Add sliced green onions to the stir-fry and toss to combine.

Optional: Sprinkle sesame seeds over the top for added flavor and presentation.

Serve the Lemon Garlic Shrimp Stir-Fry over cooked rice or noodles.

Enjoy your flavorful and zesty Lemon Garlic Shrimp Stir-Fry! It's a quick and healthy meal with vibrant colors and fresh flavors.

Roasted Brussels Sprouts and Quinoa Salad

Ingredients:

For the Salad:

- 1 cup quinoa, rinsed
- 2 cups Brussels sprouts, trimmed and halved
- 2 tablespoons olive oil
- Salt and pepper to taste
- 1/2 cup dried cranberries or raisins
- 1/3 cup chopped pecans or walnuts, toasted
- 1/4 cup crumbled feta cheese (optional)

For the Dressing:

- 3 tablespoons olive oil
- 2 tablespoons balsamic vinegar
- 1 tablespoon Dijon mustard
- 1 clove garlic, minced
- Salt and pepper to taste

Instructions:

Preheat your oven to 400°F (200°C).

Cook quinoa according to package instructions. Once cooked, fluff it with a fork and let it cool to room temperature.

Toss the halved Brussels sprouts with olive oil, salt, and pepper. Spread them in a single layer on a baking sheet.

Roast the Brussels sprouts in the preheated oven for 20-25 minutes or until they are golden brown and crispy on the edges.

While the Brussels sprouts are roasting, prepare the dressing. In a small bowl, whisk together olive oil, balsamic vinegar, Dijon mustard, minced garlic, salt, and pepper.

In a large mixing bowl, combine the cooked quinoa, roasted Brussels sprouts, dried cranberries (or raisins), and toasted nuts.

Pour the dressing over the salad and toss to combine, ensuring all ingredients are well coated.

If using, sprinkle crumbled feta cheese over the top of the salad.

Serve the Roasted Brussels Sprouts and Quinoa Salad at room temperature or chilled.

This salad is not only flavorful but also packed with protein and fiber. It makes for a great side dish or a light and satisfying main course. Enjoy!

Herb-Marinated Grilled Lamb Chops

Ingredients:

- 8 lamb chops (about 1 inch thick)
- 3 tablespoons olive oil
- 3 cloves garlic, minced
- 2 tablespoons fresh rosemary, finely chopped
- 2 tablespoons fresh thyme, finely chopped
- 1 tablespoon fresh mint, finely chopped
- Zest of 1 lemon
- Juice of 1 lemon
- Salt and black pepper to taste

Instructions:

In a bowl, combine olive oil, minced garlic, chopped rosemary, chopped thyme, chopped mint, lemon zest, lemon juice, salt, and black pepper to create the marinade.

Place the lamb chops in a large dish or a resealable plastic bag.

Pour the marinade over the lamb chops, making sure each chop is well coated. You can use a brush or your hands to rub the marinade onto the chops.

Cover the dish or seal the bag and marinate the lamb chops in the refrigerator for at least 2 hours, or ideally overnight for more flavor.

Preheat your grill to medium-high heat.

Remove the lamb chops from the refrigerator and let them come to room temperature for about 20-30 minutes.

Grill the lamb chops for about 3-4 minutes per side for medium-rare, or adjust the cooking time to your desired level of doneness.

Allow the grilled lamb chops to rest for a few minutes before serving.

Optional: Garnish with additional fresh herbs and lemon wedges before serving.

Serve these Herb-Marinated Grilled Lamb Chops with your favorite sides, such as roasted vegetables, couscous, or a fresh salad. Enjoy the delicious blend of herbs and smoky flavors!

www.ingramcontent.com/pod-product-compliance
Lightning Source LLC
LaVergne TN
LVHW081555060526
838201LV00054B/1902